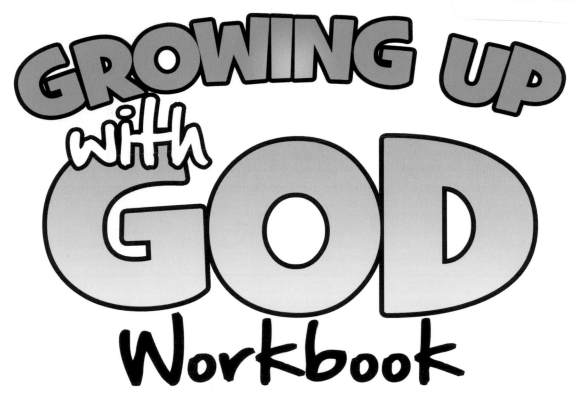

GROWING UP with GOD Workbook

SHAWN BOLZ

Illustrations | R.W. Lamont Hunt | www.dakotakidcreations.com
Cover design | Yvonne Parks | www.pearcreative.ca
Interior design | Odia Reimer | www.odiareimer.com

PREFACE

Living this life well has always been about God's love. When Jesus was first baptized by John the Baptist, God the Father spoke from heaven saying: "You are my Son, chosen and marked by my love, pride of my life" (Luke 3: 22).

Sometimes you can feel like you are doing things for God to perform for Him, and that He will love you more when you are good. Your parents don't love you because of what you can do for them. They love you because they made you and you come from them. You are their joy because you belong to them, not because you can ever do enough to make yourself more valuable. When you were a baby, you could do nothing for your parents that helped them. They had to change your diapers, feed you, rock you to sleep, and wake up with you. Yet all parents love their little babies as if they are fully valuable.

When God looks at you, He already loves you and says you are His chosen child. You are marked by His love and He is proud of you. That means you don't have to do things to earn more of His love. You get to do things because He loves you!

This workbook is about how you get to grow up with God. You get to bring the world amazing love from your heavenly Father—love that will change the world! I know you're going to enjoy the adventure.

Shawn Bolz

TABLE OF CONTENTS

Workbook
CHAPTER
1

CHILDREN'S TESTIMONY

Lucy's Testimony, Age 9

I asked one of my leaders, Rey, if he was sick or in pain. "No, but you can give me a word from God," he replied. My mom reminded me of what I had learned about hearing from God, so I listened and then looked up at him and said, "I see God advancing your career soon." Rey began to laugh and explained he had been up for a promotion for several months and it kept getting delayed. He worked with one of the very big companies in town. The very next week, he told us that he got the promotion!

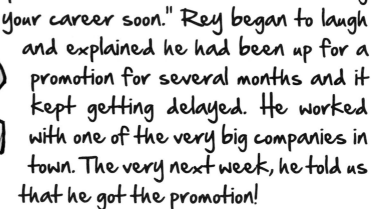

CHAPTER 1 STORY SYNOPSIS

Maria, Lucas, and Harper are at summer camp, where they've been learning about friendship with God. Maria is starting to get to know God better. Harper and Lucas are her best friends, and they are a little further along.

On the last night of the camp, their group activity is to pray with each other to hear the voice of God. Even though Maria loves summer camp, she is nervous and stressed out about this part of it because she has never really heard God's voice and is afraid she might never be able to hear Him speak to her. Lucas and Harper encourage Maria to listen to God. When she does hear something, they help her figure out what to do next. They all hear different things that encourage them on their God-journey.

CONNECT WITH GOD AS A FRIEND

TEACHING POINT 1

CONNECT WITH GOD AS A FRIEND

Did you know that God made you for friendship? God made people because He wanted to share everything He had made with them. He wanted us! He wanted friends, companions, and kids like you who He could be with all the time. We can know Him and also connect to Him! Just like a computer connects to Wi-Fi, you are connected by your spirit to the heart of God. His heart is massive! His love reaches everywhere, and it can help you live the best kind of life.

Paul said, "God can do anything, you know—far more than you could ever imagine or guess or request in your wildest dreams! He does it not by pushing us around but by working within us, His Spirit deeply and gently within us" (Ephesians 3:20). That is friendship language! God gives us His Spirit to help us connect to Him as a friend. He works deeply within us! Jesus knew that kids would understand this. You are no less important than grown-ups in the kingdom of God! He is ready to invest real time with you now!

Journal

_____

_____

_____

_____

TEACHING
POINT
I

CONNECT WITH GOD AS A FRIEND, CONTINUED...

God was thinking about you for millions of years before He ever created you. It's just like an artist who thinks about what he's going to paint for ages before he starts to paint his best creation! God spent time thinking of what you would like, what would make you happy, what kind of personality you would have, and what kinds of dreams you would dream. Thinking about spending forever with you made Him really happy.

Jesus says, "I came so they can have real and eternal life, more and better life than they ever dreamed of" (John 10:10). He said this about you! He made you. He created you to have a quality of friendship with Him that is epic. He created you to have a quality of eternal life that will be awesome—even here on earth! He made you to connect with Him as a friend, both on earth and in heaven.

Journal

_____

_____

_____

_____

_____

_____

_____

Question/Reflection

When was the first time you felt like God was your friend? What did you feel? Maybe you didn't feel anything but you just knew. How did you know?

_____

_____

_____

_____

_____

_____

_____

_____

_____

_____

_____

_____

_____

_____

_____

FRIENDSHIP WITH GOD IS INTERACTIVE

TEACHING POINT 2

FRIENDSHIP WITH GOD IS INTERACTIVE

Friendship with God is interactive, which means that you always get to share and talk with God about everything. The Bible shows us that God spent great time and energy connecting with those He loved as a good friend.

Friendships get better with friends you care about and talk to a lot. You can grow into this friendship with God and grow up with God. Jesus was always talking to God. He even said that because of the Holy Spirit in you, you would have the same kind of relationship with God that He has. That means you will hear what the Father is saying to you, too!

Journal

_____

_____

_____

_____

_____

_____

_____

_____

TEACHING POINT 2

FRIENDSHIP WITH GOD IS INTERACTIVE, CONTINUED...

Jesus even explained this to the disciples and called the Holy Spirit "the Friend." "If I don't leave, the Friend won't come. But if I go, I'll send him to you. I still have many things to tell you, but you can't handle them now. But when the Friend comes, the Spirit of the Truth, He will take you by the hand and guide you into all the truth there is. He won't draw attention to Himself, but will make sense out of what is about to happen and, indeed, out of all that I have done and said. He will honor me; he will take from me and deliver it to you. Everything the Father has is also mine. That is why I've said, 'He takes from me and delivers to you'" (John 16:7, 12-15).

Jesus spent time with God like He was a real friend, not just a person way out there or far away. What did this friendship look like? It looked like spending time together, sharing ideas with God, having fun with God. This friendship showed loyalty—sticking up for God's heart, trusting God to care for His safety and well-being, and working on the skills to keep His friendship going. When you're friends with God, you get to do stuff with Him.

Journal

_____

_____

_____

_____

Question/Reflection

The Holy Spirit was Jesus' friend, and they had a lot of fun and good conversations together. Jesus said the Holy Spirit takes from God and delivers it to you. What do you think of that?

_____

_____

_____

_____

_____

_____

_____

_____

_____

_____

_____

YOU CAN LEARN HOW TO LISTEN TO GOD

YOU CAN LEARN HOW TO LISTEN TO GOD

Jesus knew how to listen to God and so did the disciples. As a matter of fact, Jesus made it easy to understand that we all naturally hear God's voice. You were wired for it! He says that the Good Shepherd's sheep hear His voice, (John 10: 27) meaning you can hear His voice.

It takes practice to learn how to hear God in your spirit or heart. It can be hard to learn because you are expecting to hear God talk to you in the same way you hear everyone else do it. Sometimes God's voice is like the voice in your own head. Sometimes His voice is like having a brilliant idea, and sometimes it's like a beautiful picture in your head that means something to you. When you are growing up in your friendship with God, you get to learn how He talks to you!

Journal

_____

_____

_____

_____

_____

_____

_____

_____

TEACHING POINT 3

YOU CAN LEARN HOW TO LISTEN TO GOD, CONTINUED...

Maria didn't think God would talk to her. Once she was thinking about how good it felt to sing to God about her love for Him, and she saw a gentle father's face smiling. She heard, "I have made you to be creative like me. You are an actress." She heard God while she was thinking about how good God was. It surprised her and she didn't even know she could pray with Jesus to hear more. She was just excited to have heard anything! She learned how to hear God by paying attention to her thoughts and the pictures in her mind.

Journal

_____

_____

_____

_____

_____

_____

_____

_____

_____

_____

Question/Reflection

Maria was worried that she might never be able to hear God talk to her. Have you ever worried about that, too? If so, have you talked to God about it? He can always hear you. Write down anything you're nervous about when you think about hearing God talk to you.

_____

_____

_____

_____

_____

_____

_____

_____

_____

GROWTH ACTIVITY

FOR YOU

Write down three things that you think you could do more often to grow in your friendship with God. These can be things like, "Spend more time with God as a friend" or "Hear from God more."

Now ask the Holy Spirit to show you a practical step you can take toward doing one or more of these things this week, like "Every morning while I'm getting dressed, I'll ask God to show me a picture in my mind of something about my day." Write down what you hear or see.

1 _____

2 _____

3 _____

GROWTH ACTIVITY

FOR YOUR GROUP

Take turns sharing something that makes your friendship with God seem real and strong. What is the best thing about your friendship with God? Each person will then pray that blessing over everyone else in the group.

For example: "The best thing about my friendship with God is when a bird flies by me when I'm in my backyard. It's like He's sending me a gift and reminding me that He knows I love nature. I pray over all of you that same blessing of being able to see God's messages in nature."

GROWTH PRAYER

Say this out loud:

God, thank You for being a real friend to me, even when I don't see it.

I choose to be Your real friend.

Help me to interact with You in real ways, like friends do.

Would You show me how You talk to me and teach me how to listen to Your voice?

Thank You.
Amen!

Workbook
CHAPTER
2

CHILDREN'S TESTIMONY

Sophie's Testimony, Age 9

I saw the leader, Johnny, at camp, except he wasn't the age he is now; he was a young boy. I saw him waking up one morning. I could see his room and everything in his room. Bed, dresser, desk—everything you'd see in a normal room. I saw a gold straw hat sitting on the dresser, and it stood out to me. I saw him with this gold straw hat, and he loved it and wore it all the time; he wouldn't go anywhere without it. I asked him if he wanted to make stuff like that. He said he used to want to be a fashion model, and that was a real gold straw hat that he loved a lot. I think the Lord loved that he wanted to be a fashion model, and He was bringing that up for him again.

CHAPTER 2 STORY SYNOPSIS

Lucas gets home from camp and shares, with his mom, all about what God did. He shares how Harper, Maria, and he prayed to hear God talk to them about their lives. He then tells his mom about his personal prophecy from the guest minister, and that it was all about being kind and helping others have a kind nature. His mom understands, because God has helped her grow in love and compassion over the years, too. She encourages him by telling him that God has already started growing him in those ways. She's happy about what has happened to him spiritually, which helps Lucas to value it all even more.

Lucas treasures the prophetic word he received and also what God showed him personally. He thinks it all over in his heart and tells God he's ready to learn everything God wants him to learn about compassion and love.

GO ON A GOD JOURNEY WITH YOUR CLOSE FRIENDS AND FAMILY

TEACHING
POINT
4

GO ON A GOD JOURNEY
WITH YOUR CLOSE FRIENDS
AND FAMILY

God loves to share His heart with you. He can do this when you read the Bible or when you are just experiencing Him with your friends. Sometimes His talking to you sounds like thoughts in your head or heart, and sometimes you can hear His voice. He is constantly nudging you to see things. He points out people around you. He points them out so you can love them the same way He does, if you will just learn to recognize that it is Him talking.

When God speaks to you, He loves it when you celebrate His words with your friends or family. Many times this is how He can tell you even more. Your friends and family will have insights, prayers, and encouragement for you so that you can learn more about what God is showing you. It's like when your parents or sports coaches help you in your sports journey. They help to celebrate when you do amazingly well, but also encourage and support you when it is tough. No athlete can become amazing without a community of coaches, friends, and family around.

Journal

_____

_____

_____

_____

_____

TEACHING POINT 4

GO ON A GOD JOURNEY WITH YOUR CLOSE FRIENDS AND FAMILY, CONTINUED...

Friends and family can help remind you of who you are when you're having a tough time. They can tell you when something God tells you happens, or when someone's prophecy to you gets fulfilled. They will help celebrate it with you! We all get excited about what God did or is doing, and we worship Him and celebrate Him working in one another. "Let's keep a firm grip on the promises that keep us going. He always keeps His word. Let's see how inventive we can be in encouraging love and helping out, not avoiding worshiping together as some do but spurring each other on, especially as we see the big Day approaching" (Hebrews 10:23-25).

This also happens when you share with your friends what you are reading in Scripture and you apply it together. Psalm 119:105 says, "By your words I can see where I'm going; they throw a beam of light on my dark path." This means that God's Word helps to guide you in relationships and life's decisions!

Journal

_____
_____
_____
_____

Question/Reflection

Lucas's mom was excited to hear Lucas talk about his word from God. She encouraged him and told him he was special. How can you encourage and help others get more connected to God?

_____

_____

_____

_____

_____

_____

_____

_____

_____

_____

_____

_____

_____

TREASURE WHAT GOD TELLS YOU

TREASURE WHAT GOD TELLS YOU

God tells you things so that you can know what He is going to do in you and through you. It helps to build your confidence and your faith, and you get to see which areas you need to grow in. When the angel came and told Mary about baby Jesus and that she would be His mom, she was in awe of God's love and respect toward her. She was amazed that He picked her. She had a lot to think about! Luke says, "But Mary treasured up all these things and pondered them in her heart" (Luke 2:19).

When you ponder something in your heart, it means you're always aware of it. You always know it's there. It means carrying around what God has said to you as though it's about to happen at any moment. You don't let it leave your thoughts. Instead you make sure God's words and promises are always a part of how you see your day and your life. That's what Lucas did. He heard the word "brother." He didn't know what God was telling him about, but he pondered it and asked God about it. He knew it was a mystery that God would explain and make happen in the future, and he chose to keep his heart connected to the word.

Journal

_____

_____

_____

_____

TEACHING POINT 5

TREASURE WHAT GOD TELLS YOU, CONTINUED...

Have you ever wanted a new toy and knew that if you asked for it for Christmas or your birthday, you would probably get it? If you knew that, then every day you would think about the enjoyment of getting that toy until it came! You can do exactly the same thing with what God tells you. You can think about it every day and smile, knowing that God loves to make His promises come true!

Journal

_____

_____

_____

_____

_____

_____

_____

_____

_____

_____

_____

_____

_____

Question/Reflection

Do you treasure the things God has told you? Do you think about them when you are making decisions about your life? It's important to do! What are some things you could do to help you remember?

_____

_____

_____

_____

_____

_____

_____

_____

_____

_____

_____

HELP OTHERS HAVE FAITH TO CONNECT TO GOD

TEACHING POINT 6

HELP OTHERS HAVE FAITH TO CONNECT TO GOD

On your spiritual journey you learn how God speaks to you. One of the amazing things that happens is that your growing connection to God helps you encourage everyone else with theirs!

We are supposed to be creative in how we can help other Christians grow in God. Remember what Paul said earlier in this chapter? "Let's see how inventive we can be in encouraging love and helping out, not avoiding worshiping together as some do but spurring each other on, especially as we see the big Day approaching" (Hebrews 10:25). God shows us how much He loves us in so many different ways each day. He's very creative about coming up with ways to help us get to know His heart better. You can be as creative as He is.

Journal

_____

_____

_____

_____

_____

_____

_____

TEACHING POINT 6

HELP OTHERS HAVE FAITH TO CONNECT TO GOD, CONTINUED...

Lucas's mom was excited to hear Lucas talk about his word from God. It probably reminded her about some of the ways God had fulfilled His promises for her own life. By encouraging him, she was encouraging her own faith, too.

Isn't that amazing? You get to spur others on with the love that you feel from God and the excitement you have about seeing His promises happen. Another way of looking at it is that your stories of what God does with you help to create faith in other people. They start to believe that they will have their own stories with God, too. It is like receiving a power-up in a video game—you grow when you hear. In Romans 10:17, Paul says that faith comes by hearing about Jesus.

Journal

_____

_____

_____

_____

_____

_____

_____

Question/Reflection

God made you to be creative about coming up with ways to connect with His heart. If you stop and think about that right now, what are some things you could start doing to connect to Him more?

_____

_____

_____

_____

_____

_____

_____

_____

_____

_____

_____

GROWTH ACTIVITY

FOR YOU

Write a letter to God and remind Him of all the things you believe about Him, or list the things you believe He has told you that you will get to do in life. Write down at least five things that you are dreaming will happen in your future, or that you feel you were made to do.

_____

_____

_____

_____

_____

_____

_____

_____

_____

GROWTH ACTIVITY

FOR YOUR GROUP

Practice encouragement: Sharing your dreams or the messages you feel God has given you is a vulnerable process. In this group time, have people take turns sharing something they are dreaming about doing in their lifetimes. Then the group will pray for the person sharing and encourage him or her about this dream. For example: Person 1 says, "I want to be a nurse." The group then prays or says words of encouragement over that person. "You are very nurturing! You take care of people well! I pray that God would give you understanding about how to pursue that goal."

GROWTH PRAYER

God, help me to share my spiritual journey in real ways with my family and friends!

Help me to treasure what You tell me like Mary did!

Also, help me spur my friends and family on to grow with You, too!

Amen!

Workbook
CHAPTER

3

CHILDREN'S TESTIMONY

Sarah's Testimony, Age 5

When I was around five years old and my middle brother was nearly four, we had this incredible encounter with the Holy Spirit. All of a sudden, we knew that Jesus was in the room with us and His Spirit was burning inside us. We danced like never before, then fell to the ground in praise and prayer. In those moments, we both clearly heard God say (in our hearts and thoughts), "I want you two to be dance teachers in the church. My people need to know how to dance like this and enjoy Me." We were jumping up and down, doing cartwheels, shouting, and celebrating!

The thing is, we're both awful dancers, but God wanted us to dance with Him with all our hearts and not be afraid of what we looked like while we were doing it. Since then, we've found that it's easy for us to help draw people into God's presence. They can play with Him joyfully and be confident and alive in their worship times with Him.

CHAPTER 3 STORY SYNOPSIS

Maria tries to join a drama class at the local theater because of the word about acting that she thought God gave her, but the class is full! Maria is very discouraged because she thinks the only way the word will happen is if she takes acting classes. She wonders if she heard God at all. Harper's mom invites Maria to join the choir class at the theater with Harper, which is fun, but not the same thing to Maria.

Lucas, Harper, and Maria practice hearing God again that night. Maria very clearly hears God give her a word for Lucas's grandmother. Harper tells Maria that if God cares that much about Lucas's grandmother having faith about selling her house, then maybe she can have faith that He's going to make her word come true, too. Maria agrees and feels like her faith has grown.

GOD HAS A BIGGER PICTURE IN MIND WHEN HE TELLS YOU THINGS

GOD HAS A BIGGER PICTURE IN MIND WHEN HE TELLS YOU THINGS

When you start to hear from God, you will realize that what He says and what you think aren't always the same. He sometimes speaks in pictures, parables, or stories to communicate a thought to you. This is because He doesn't just want to tell you what to do. He also wants you to know His heart. Have you ever tried to tell a friend something, and had to use a story or picture of what you mean in order to really get it across? "That was as awesome as the first time I won a prize!" This communicates how excited you are and how deeply something impacted you.

God is like this, too. He doesn't just talk so you can hear what He is saying. He talks to show you what He is feeling too. When He gives you a message or a word about something He wants to do in your life, He's going to make it happen His way. He wants to do something for you that only He can do. That means you can't do it on your own or with your own abilities, even if they are good ones. This way you know it's Him and not you making it happen. Whenever God is doing something in you or for you, it is also for the world around you. He loves the world, and He uses your life to bring others the truth of His love.

Journal

_____

_____

_____

TEACHING POINT 7

GOD HAS A BIGGER PICTURE IN MIND WHEN HE TELLS YOU THINGS, CONTINUED...

"Take a good look, friends, at who you were when you got called into this life. I don't see many of 'the brightest and the best' among you, not many influential, not many from high-society families. Isn't it obvious that God deliberately chose men and women that the culture overlooks and exploits and abuses, chose these 'nobodies' to expose the hollow pretensions of the 'somebodies'? That makes it quite clear that none of you can get by with blowing your own horn before God" (1 Corinthians 1:26-29).

In other words, God didn't choose you because you were the best or give you great purpose because you are so skilled. He chose you knowing you couldn't be you without Him! You make Him look good. When you try something beyond your ability, just because you have faith that God wants it and will help get it done, you look like Jesus!

Journal

_____

_____

_____

_____

_____

_____

Question/Reflection

When God gives you a word or tells you something about the future, why do you think He usually makes those things happen in ways you don't expect?

_____

_____

_____

_____

_____

_____

_____

_____

_____

_____

_____

_____

_____

YOUR PROCESS IS SOMETIMES DIFFERENT FROM EVERYONE ELSE'S

YOUR PROCESS IS SOMETIMES DIFFERENT FROM EVERYONE ELSE'S

You want God to work in your life and to grow your heart to be as big as His. That means you are asking for the impossible! It also means your process—the way God does that in you—isn't always the same way He does it in everyone else.

You might even be pursuing the same dreams as people who aren't saved, but you're not doing it for the same reasons they are! Many Christian kids compare themselves to their non-Christian friends and wonder why their process isn't as easy or as direct. Galatians 6:4-5 says, "Make a careful exploration of who you are and the work you have been given, and then sink yourself into that. Don't be impressed with yourself. Don't compare yourself with others. Each of you must take responsibility for doing the creative best you can with your own life."

Journal

_____

_____

_____

_____

_____

_____

_____

YOUR PROCESS IS SOMETIMES DIFFERENT FROM EVERYONE ELSE'S, CONTINUED...

Well, you are not asking for the same results or life they are. You are asking for a spiritual and abundantly crazy, awesome life of character and good works! That means your process will be different. Jesus kept looking at the Father in heaven as His only model for how to do things. He didn't look at the people around Him. When you are walking with God, you get to learn that sometimes He won't pick a predictable way of doing things. That's because He wants you and the world around you to know that He is with you! He works in your life and causes things to happen that you couldn't do alone.

You will find that sometimes you receive an upgrade from God, much like your computer or smart device gets a new update. This happens when God shares His heart with you or when a part of the Bible comes alive in you. You have more to work with than before, even if it's only more faith.

Journal

_____

_____

_____

_____

_____

Question/Reflection

What kind of spiritual upgrades has God already given you? What has He done in your life and in your heart that has made you feel more connected to Him?

_____

_____

_____

_____

_____

_____

_____

_____

_____

_____

_____

_____

_____

GOD CAN SHOW YOU WHAT IS POSSIBLE THROUGH OTHERS

TEACHING
POINT
9

GOD CAN SHOW YOU WHAT IS POSSIBLE THROUGH OTHERS

It is possible to be like Jesus because He said you will do greater works than He did. "Believe me: I am in my Father and my Father is in me. If you can't believe that, believe what you see—these works. The person who trusts me will not only do what I'm doing but even greater things, because I, on my way to the Father, am giving you the same work to do that I've been doing. You can count on it" (John 14:11-12).

Brothers and sisters always want to have what's fair, and parents try their hardest to make sure that they never give more to one child than another. Because we're all God's children, when you see God doing something for someone else, it gives you a receipt that you can cash in with the Father. You should always want the same benefits you see others getting, even if that benefit will end up making your life turn out differently than your friends' lives. Every benefit God gives you will be super valuable.

Journal

_____

_____

_____

_____

_____

_____

GOD CAN SHOW YOU WHAT IS POSSIBLE THROUGH OTHERS, CONTINUED...

Romans 2:11 says: "God doesn't give based on where you are from or how you were brought up." God doesn't play favorites. He doesn't like one of us more than another. He doesn't do something for one of His kids that he isn't willing to do for another. He didn't just send Jesus for some of us! He sent Him for all of us, so we could all be restored to Him! This means you have full access to what God wants to provide for you. You should get spiritually hungry for what God has done for your friends so he can do it for you.

Journal

_____

_____

_____

_____

_____

_____

_____

_____

_____

Question/Reflection

What examples have you seen in your own life and in your friends' lives to prove that God wants to bless everyone with a close connection to His heart?

_____

_____

_____

_____

_____

_____

_____

_____

_____

_____

_____

_____

_____

_____

GROWTH ACTIVITY

FOR YOU

Read example 1 and choose a person who fits the description. Write their name in box 1 and tell why you chose them. Do numbers 2 and 3 the same way.

1) Someone who has a career you'd like to have someday, or someone who is happy in a career the way you want to be. Write down what inspires and excites you about that job.

2) Someone who loves God the way you want to love God.

3) The person who has impacted you the most in your life.

Now turn on a worship song and let God encourage your heart for five minutes about all the awesome ways He will help you be you. He's already done it for the three people you listed. Imagine who you get to be as you grow in God.

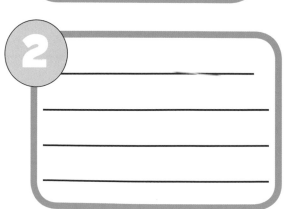

GROWTH ACTIVITY

FOR YOUR GROUP

Have three of the group members share what their hobbies are. Then have three group members share what their favorite type of movie or TV show is. Then have three members share about the way they became a Christian. Isn't it amazing that our processes are completely different, and yet we are all the same?

GROWTH PRAYER

God, I know that You always have a full picture in mind when You tell me something, and I trust You!

My process may be different from everyone else's, but it is because You and I want a different result than theirs!

When I see You bless someone else with heart growth or an opportunity to grow toward seeing their dream come true, help me to want and believe that You will do the same for me, too.

Amen!

Workbook
CHAPTER
4

CHILDREN'S TESTIMONY

Will's Story, Age 9

There was a kid at school who kept bullying me. We did everything: my parents talked to the principal and the teachers, and they talked to his parents. Then one day, God gave me a vision of who he was, and I saw him the way God loves him. I felt like God said he loved the same kinds of books I did. So I brought one to school the next day with a note that said, "I forgive you for being mean to me and hope that you enjoy this book. I am a Christian and asked God what you liked, and I felt like He told me this book was something you liked, so I wanted to give it to you. This is my favorite book series, so if you want to talk about it later, we can."

He told me the next day that he had been wanting that book forever, and we ended up talking all about it. Now he is my best friend, and I know—from him telling me— that he had been going through a real hard time in life when he was being mean to me.

CHAPTER 4 STORY SYNOPSIS

Lucas goes to the first soccer practice of the season. The kids start picking on a new kid, and Lucas feels he has to intervene. He does, but then the bully starts making fun of Lucas and pushes him to the ground as well. It doesn't bother Lucas, but later as he talks to the new kid, Jamal, he starts to feel the presence of the Holy Spirit. He thinks that his word from God about having a brother might apply to a new friendship with Jamal. This seems strange to him, because he doesn't even know Jamal.

Lucas takes a risk on what he thinks the word means. He asks Jamal to hang out even though Lucas wasn't really looking for a new friend. After the conversation, Lucas spends a lot of time thinking about what God is going to do next.

RECOGNIZE THE PRESENCE OF GOD AND TAKE CHANCES

TEACHING POINT 10

RECOGNIZE THE PRESENCE OF GOD AND TAKE CHANCES

Learning how to grow in your relationship with God happens at all times. You learn as much through your time with other kids or on projects as you do when you are praying or at a church meeting. It is good to process your day with God every night before you go to bed. Is there anything He is highlighting to you that you did well in? Celebrate that and thank God for it. Was there anything you regret that you did or said? Just say sorry to God and think about how you will do it differently next time. Dwell on what was good throughout your day or week.

Sometimes doing things God's told you to do, through the Holy Spirit or the Bible, can cost you something. You have to take chances that not every other kid would take, like befriending a bullied kid or helping someone through a hard time. Jesus was always doing this. He was the most important person on earth, and yet He stopped to play with kids and hang out with people no one else would. He was a friend to everyone.

Journal

_____

_____

_____

_____

_____

TEACHING POINT 10

RECOGNIZE THE PRESENCE OF GOD AND TAKE CHANCES, CONTINUED...

Jesus preached one of His most amazing messages about you: "Let me tell you why you are here. You're here to be salt-seasoning that brings out the God-flavors of this earth. If you lose your saltiness, how will people taste godliness? . . . You're here to be light, bringing out the God-colors in the world. God is not a secret to be kept. . . . Be generous with your lives. By opening up to others, you'll prompt people to open up with God, this generous Father in heaven" (Matthew 5: 13-16).

You are called to show the world what He is like. Sometimes this means taking a risk by spending time with someone who no one else will spend time with, or by doing something nice for someone when you don't even know him or her. When you are a light like this, God causes you to shine from brighter and brighter places, and He is so proud of you.

Journal

_____

_____

_____

_____

_____

Question/Reflection

Is there anything you are afraid might happen if you are brave and do what God asks you to do? What would make you less afraid?

_____

_____

_____

_____

_____

_____

_____

_____

_____

_____

_____

_____

_____

_____

TAKE SMALL STEPS OF RISK TO START GROWING

TAKE SMALL STEPS OF RISK TO START GROWING

When you are learning how to walk with God and hear His voice, you just have to take one step at a time. We all have to start somewhere. If you heard God say you are called to love homeless people, maybe your mom can help you pack a lunch for a homeless person you see sometimes and bring it to him. The only way to grow in faith is by action.

James talks about this: "Dear friends, do you think you'll get anywhere in this if you learn all the right words but never do anything? Does merely talking about faith indicate that a person really has it? For instance, you come upon an old friend dressed in rags and half-starved and say, 'Good morning, friend! Be clothed in Christ! Be filled with the Holy Spirit!' and walk off without providing so much as a coat or a cup of soup—where does that get you? Isn't it obvious that God-talk without God-acts is outrageous nonsense? . . . You can no more show me your works apart from your faith than I can show you my faith apart from my works. Faith and works, works and faith, fit together hand in glove" (James 2:14-17).

Journal

_____

_____

_____

_____

TEACHING POINT II

TAKE SMALL STEPS OF RISK TO START GROWING, CONTINUED...

When God speaks to you and when you do what He says, you should be able to track the difference He's made in your life. You should be able to see the difference you are making in the world around you. Maybe it's as simple as an act of service for your parents by doing dishes or walking the dog. Maybe it's as intense as joining a program at school to volunteer with disabled kids. The reality is that you will only grow in God when you take steps of faith to do something that comes out of your relationship with Him. Lots of people say they are mature in their relationship with God because they know a lot, but knowing a lot without a friendship with God is a dead relationship.

Journal

_____

_____

_____

_____

_____

_____

_____

_____

Question/Reflection

What small steps can you take this week that will help you grow in love? If you have already done some kind acts, what difference have you seen them make in the lives of those around you?

_____

_____

_____

_____

_____

_____

_____

_____

_____

_____

_____

_____

BE ON THE LOOKOUT FOR WAYS TO APPLY WORDS TO CURRENT CIRCUMSTANCES

BE ON THE LOOKOUT FOR WAYS TO APPLY WORDS TO CURRENT CIRCUMSTANCES

The Bible is awesome because it teaches you how to thrive in life. Hearing God's voice and walking with Him in friendship will teach you how to be the greatest version of yourself that you were meant to be!

You have to learn to apply what He is saying to your life, though. When you are reading the Bible or listening to God and He shows you something about yourself or the world around you, write it down. Then look for it happening in your everyday life.

Journal

_____

_____

_____

_____

_____

_____

_____

_____

_____

_____

TEACHING POINT 12

BE ON THE LOOKOUT FOR WAYS TO APPLY WORDS TO CURRENT CIRCUMSTANCES, CONTINUED...

"So, chosen by God for this new life of love, dress in the wardrobe God picked out for you: compassion, kindness, humility, quiet strength, discipline. Be even-tempered, content with second place, quick to forgive an offense....And regardless of what else you put on, wear love. It's your basic, all-purpose garment. Never be without it" (Colossians 3:12-14).

Is He telling you that He is going to teach you about leadership? Look for ways to be a leader at school or with friends, in ideas or activities. Do you care about making things fair for people who are down on their luck? Jesus always stood up for the outcast. Look for ways to be kind to people whom other people ignore. As you do these things, you will definitely begin to understand how God is moving, around you and in you, to form His love in you.

Journal

_____

_____

_____

_____

_____

_____

QUESTION/REFLECTION

Question/Reflection

When you look at your Christian friends' lives, when do you see them acting like Jesus? How do you think they grow into being more like Him?

_____

_____

_____

_____

_____

_____

_____

_____

_____

_____

_____

_____

_____

WORKBOOK CHAPTER 4   75

GROWTH ACTIVITY

FOR YOU

Take a risk: Talk to someone and share something encouraging! Find someone who is safe for you to talk to and share something incredibly kind or encouraging. It can be a spiritual word or just a natural encouragement, for example: "Your smile makes the whole room feel happy," or "The way you keep trying makes me want to try harder, too. Thank you."

GROWTH ACTIVITY

FOR YOUR GROUP

Have volunteers take turns to be in the middle of the group. These should be people who feel like God has shown them something they are going to do in life but they haven't started yet, or who have something that they want to do. Now have everyone else do listening prayer (including them) to ask God for some steps or what a strategy might be to start doing that thing. Try not to give just good advice; ask Jesus!

GROWTH PRAYER

God, I pray that I would learn how to recognize Your presence.

I pray that You would give me the courage to take chances on what I think You're saying, even when it costs me something!

Help me to take risks so that I can really grow.

Help me to know how to apply Your Bible, and the words You have given me, to my everyday life.

Amen!

Workbook
CHAPTER
5

CHILDREN'S TESTIMONY

Burt's Testimony, A Grown-Up

I often take the entire children's ministry out to walk the neighborhood and pray. One particularly beautiful Sunday morning, I had the kids line up, gave them instructions, and off they went. The children had been practicing hearing from God and activating their faith and spiritual gifts. As they walked through a few blocks, praying for the city and the families that lived in the homes they were passing, they adamantly began asking to stop at this one particular house. To me, this house appeared no different than the rest. The children insisted they wanted to knock on the door and pray for whomever answered. They were compelled to give a blessing to the people inside.

I knocked at the door and a woman answered. After explaining what we had been doing and why we were there, the woman asked the children if they wanted to come inside. She allowed them to walk around and pray for God's love and safety to fill the house. After hearing their prayers, she was very moved and confided the house's true purpose. It was a secret safe place for children whose own homes weren't a safe place to be anymore. We loved that a very present and sovereign God cares for children so much that He would make sure they had a safe place to go to. It was a powerful encounter shared with that woman, the children, and our leadership team. It was incredible to see such innocent children used so easily to bring hope to a house where scared children could be safe.

CHAPTER 5 STORY SYNOPSIS

Maria finds out she and Harper are going to be in a show choir, not just a normal choir. Also a teacher has moved from New York City to host a musical in the theater next season. They will need kid actors for it, and their choir group will get to audition. Maria feels like it's her chance to be a real actress, and Harper is just as excited as Maria is about God's word to her coming true.

Maria sings really well, but then competition comes in the form of a very professional girl, Brooke, who has been singing and acting for years. Maria is devastated because there is only one lead role, and Brooke will probably get it. When Maria talks to God about her dream and word, she sees that, to God, acting is not her destiny. The people she gets to love through acting are her destiny. She gets to love like Jesus loved.

SOMETIMES GOD LEADS YOU TO YOUR GOALS IN INDIRECT WAYS

TEACHING POINT 13

SOMETIMES GOD LEADS YOU TO YOUR GOALS IN INDIRECT WAYS

Many times when God talks to you, you don't know exactly what He means until you watch Him make it happen in your life. When He tells you something, He's not just informing you of it. He wants to give you the ability to be like Him. He wants to teach you how to be amazing and how to make awesome choices. If you only do all the right things for Him, you are more of a servant than a son or daughter. God doesn't just want servants who know how to do all the right things, though. He wants sons and daughters who know how to make powerful decisions that make their Father in heaven look amazing!

"If I speak with human eloquence and angelic ecstasy but don't love, I'm nothing but the creaking of a rusty gate. If I speak God's Word with power, revealing all his mysteries and making everything plain as day, and if I have faith that says to a mountain, 'Jump,' and it jumps, but I don't love, I'm nothing" (I Corinthians 13:1-2). So if you know how to do all the right things because you have all the right principles, it's not enough. He wants you to be really connected to His heart of love because that is when you know you are really living and growing in God.

Journal

_____

_____

_____

TEACHING POINT 13

SOMETIMES GOD LEADS YOU TO YOUR GOALS IN INDIRECT WAYS, CONTINUED...

This is why Jesus told parables and stories, instead of just telling people what to do. He didn't want servants; He wanted co-heirs. He wanted to give His Father sons and daughters, not just slaves, so He told them stories that would make the kingdom come alive inside them, instead of just giving them rules they could follow.

Journal

_____

_____

_____

_____

_____

_____

_____

_____

_____

_____

_____

Question/Reflection

How does it feel different in your heart when you do things for your parents out of obedience, compared to when you do things for them out of love? Which way makes you feel more connected?

_____

_____

_____

_____

_____

_____

_____

_____

_____

_____

SOMETIMES LIFE HAS OBSTACLES IN THE WAY OF YOUR PROMISES

TEACHING POINT 14

SOMETIMES LIFE HAS OBSTACLES IN THE WAY OF YOUR PROMISES

When you hear from God about something in your future or about your life purpose, there will inevitably be obstacles that get in the way of that happening. God wants to do things, through you, that are bigger than you could do on your own. He also wants to do things in your life for different reasons than you might want. Most people, that don't know God, want to do amazing things just so other people will tell them they're amazing. If you are an awesome singer, you can make albums and buy a big house and be famous. But when God calls you to amazing things, it's so you can have an amazing impact on the world through His love! You aren't doing it for your own benefit, even though you will benefit. You are doing it for His love. The end result of you living out your life purpose will look different than it might for others. This happens because living life in God's love will give you treasure in heaven, not just fulfillment on earth!

Journal

_____

_____

_____

_____

_____

TEACHING POINT 14

SOMETIMES LIFE HAS OBSTACLES IN THE WAY OF YOUR PROMISES, CONTINUED...

Because you are not just doing things for yourself, but for God and the world around you, you will experience different obstacles than some people. If you were doing things just to make your life better, you wouldn't worry about how you affect the people around you. You might even treat people really badly to accomplish more and get what you want. As a Christian, you're here to do everything in your life to love the world and to honor God! That means that you get to treasure people, but sometimes these very people become obstacles until God unfolds His plan.

Journal

_____

_____

_____

_____

_____

_____

_____

_____

Question/Reflection

Was there ever a time when it looked like God wasn't doing what He'd promised, but then it turned out He was making it happen all along?

_____

_____

_____

_____

_____

_____

_____

_____

_____

_____

_____

_____

YOU ARE ALWAYS CALLED TO THE WHO, NOT THE WHAT

TEACHING POINT 15

YOU ARE ALWAYS CALLED TO THE WHO, NOT THE WHAT

Do you know that when Jesus was about to go to the cross, He stressed out beforehand and asked the Father to make it happen another way? But there was no other way. The Father in heaven was good, though, and showed Jesus a vision of everyone who would ever love Him. Hebrews 12:2 (NIV) says, "For the joy set before Him He went to the cross."

You were and are the joy set before Jesus. He was able to go through one of the most brutal sufferings in history because He loved you and wanted to spend eternity with you. You are called to do some amazing things in life, but sometimes you will have to work hard and even persevere through some obstacles. Have you ever asked God to show you the people you get to love so that you can endure anything? When you have love in your heart for the "who" you are performing for, then you can make it through anything! When you are just doing things because you want to perform, then you might lose hope.

Journal

_____

_____

_____

_____

_____

_____

TEACHING POINT 15

YOU ARE ALWAYS CALLED TO THE WHO, NOT THE WHAT, CONTINUED...

John talks about practicing real love when living your life. When you know who you are called to love, you can live a life full of real purpose and you will be truly living. "My dear children, let's not just talk about love; let's practice real love. This is the only way we'll know we're living truly, living in God's reality. . . .We're able to stretch our hands out and receive what we asked for because we're doing what he said, doing what pleases him. Again, this is God's command: to believe in his personally named Son, Jesus Christ. He told us to love each other, in line with the original command. As we keep his commands, we live deeply and surely in him, and he lives in us. And this is how we experience his deep and abiding presence in us: by the Spirit he gave us" (1 John 3:18-24).

Journal

_____

_____

_____

_____

_____

_____

_____

Question/Reflection

If you did nothing the right way ever again, would God still love you and want to bless you? (See Ephesians 2:8-10) That's the kind of love He wants to give you for other people.

_____

_____

_____

_____

_____

_____

_____

_____

_____

_____

GROWTH ACTIVITY

FOR YOU

Do you know what you are called to do? If you don't, ask God, your parents, and a friend what they think would be a good fit for you. This might not be the final thing you end up with, but it might give you a good idea. Ask God which groups of people you will get to love well (write this down), and ask Him for His love for them.

_____

_____

_____

_____

_____

_____

_____

_____

GROWTH ACTIVITY

FOR YOUR GROUP

Have all the people in your group take turns sharing something they want to do in life. For example: a career, ministry, hobby, or trip. Then think of people they might get to love or reach through that. Try to see a big picture in your mind of all the people you'll get to love or reach with your life. Now you can see how much love you'll need from God's heart to do it, and see how big His plan is for your life!

GROWTH PRAYER

God, when I am pursuing You, help me to trust that You are leading me even when it doesn't feel direct!

Help me to understand how to overcome any obstacle that is in the way of my spiritual promises!

Help me to see the ones I get to love . . . show me who they are . . . not just what I am supposed to do for You.

Amen!

Workbook
CHAPTER
6

CHILDREN'S TESTIMONY

Anna's Testimony, Age 4

I saw Jesus in our kitchen. My mommy had taken me and Hudson to the pool that morning, but when we had to leave the pool, I got really mad and yelled at my mom. My mom yelled back at me. After we got home and Mommy was giving us lunch, I told Mommy I was sorry I said mean words that hurt her. I know my words have power and they hurt her heart. Then my mommy asked me why I was grinning, so I told her it was because Jesus just walked in and thanked me for saying I was sorry.

Mommy said, "Jesus is here in the kitchen?" So I said, "Yes, Mommy, He is standing right next to you. Miss Dawn said that you can have Christ-ray vision, too, if you try." Mommy said she couldn't see Jesus, so she closed her eyes and said she felt Him standing next to her. We both started to cry because we were so happy.

CHAPTER 6 STORY SYNOPSIS

Lucas likes Jamal, but none of his friends do because he gets upset easily and never seems to like anyone. Lucas asks God to help him love Jamal well. He's finding it hard to understand why God wants him to be his friend when he's not that easy to be around.

Lucas invites him on a boys' night with his dad, and Jamal has a great time. Afterwards, he shares how he is a foster kid and his home life has been very difficult. Both Lucas and his dad have a strong sense of compassion for him because of his situation. Lucas's parents help Lucas understand that God wants him to see Jamal the way God made him to be, and to look past his flaws. As Christians, we get to do this for everyone. We get to love each other into being the way God designed us to be.

LISTEN TO GOD, EVEN WHEN WHAT HE TELLS YOU TO DO IS HARD

LISTEN TO GOD, EVEN WHEN WHAT HE TELLS YOU TO DO IS HARD

You need to press into listening to God and praying even when it's hard. He is always with you and wants to help you connect to His heart. Sometimes it can be very hard to do what God is asking you to do. Jesus said His road is narrow. This can mean that sometimes it's not easy for you to follow God because there isn't as much freedom for you to be selfish or to just do normal things. If you want a different result, then you have to live a different way.

"Enter through the narrow gate. For wide is the gate and broad is the road that leads to destruction, and many enter through it. But small is the gate and narrow the road that leads to life, and only a few find it. Learning to trust God when we are walking with him is essential!" (Matthew 7:13-14 NIV). "Trust God from the bottom of your heart; don't try to figure out everything on your own. Listen for God's voice in everything you do, everywhere you go; he's the one who will keep you on track" (Proverbs 3:5-6).

Journal

_____

_____

_____

_____

TEACHING POINT 16

LISTEN TO GOD, EVEN WHEN WHAT HE TELLS YOU TO DO IS HARD, CONTINUED...

When Lucas began to be friends with Jamal, it wasn't easy. Jamal was changing, but it felt slow and other kids didn't want to be around him. Lucas only stayed friends with Jamal because he felt God's love and friendship for him, not because it was extremely satisfying. He was waiting for God to make them like brothers, like He'd promised. It took awhile before this happened. Galatians 6:9 says, "Let's not allow ourselves to get fatigued doing good. At the right time we will harvest a good crop if we don't give up, or quit." This means that if you keep going in faith, you will get everything God has promised. It will be like walking in an apple orchard and finding that every apple is ready to be picked and eaten.

You also need to learn how to listen to God's voice encourage you when it is hard. People who just try to do what is right just to fit in often miss out on intimacy with God. He wants to encourage you and show you that He is with you.

Journal

_____

_____

_____

_____

Question/Reflection

What do you think Matthew 7:13-14 means, to "enter through the narrow gate?" The narrow gate "leads to life, and only a few find it." Why do you think it's so important to Jesus that we do things His way?

_____

_____

_____

_____

_____

_____

_____

_____

_____

_____

SEE WHAT HE IS DOING IN OR THROUGH YOUR LIFE

TEACHING POINT 17

SEE WHAT HE IS DOING IN OR THROUGH YOUR LIFE

Even the disciples had to learn and grow. Jesus was preaching and telling them stories all the time, and they almost always had to ask Him to explain the meaning behind the stories. He was used to their questions, and often, instead of answering them directly, He actually told them more stories! He wasn't trying to just build their knowledge or intellect. He was teaching them how to see everything through love.

After three years of being with Him, the disciples had grown in love and had formed a heart connection with Him: "His disciples said, 'Finally! You're giving it to us straight, in plain talk—no more figures of speech. Now we know that you know everything—it all comes together in you. You won't have to put up with our questions anymore'" (John 16:29). Who changed? Did Jesus change or the disciples? This Scripture should help you so much! Jesus is going to mature you so that you really understand what He is talking about and your heart has grown in love!

Journal

_____

_____

_____

_____

_____

TEACHING POINT 17

SEE WHAT HE IS DOING IN OR THROUGH YOUR LIFE, CONTINUED...

When people read the Bible to you or tell you spiritual things that are amazing to them, it doesn't always excite you as much as when you discover it yourself. It is like when you hear all about a new kid at school. It may make you interested in meeting him or her, but you are not about to become friends until you spend time with the kid yourself.

The more time Solomon spent with God, the wiser he became: "God gave Solomon wisdom—the deepest of understanding and the largest of hearts. There was nothing beyond him, nothing he couldn't handle.... Sent by kings from all over the earth who had heard of his reputation, people came from far and near to listen to the wisdom of Solomon" (1 Kings 4:29-34). You aren't growing well spiritually until you discover God for yourself.

Journal

_____

_____

_____

_____

_____

_____

Question/Reflection

Sometimes we can get tired waiting for God to do what He's promised. What can you do to keep trusting Him and doing what He wants you to do?

_____

_____

_____

_____

_____

_____

_____

_____

_____

_____

_____

_____

_____

GOD IS ALWAYS TEACHING YOU AND SHARING HIMSELF WITH YOU

TEACHING POINT 18

GOD IS ALWAYS TEACHING YOU AND SHARING HIMSELF WITH YOU

When you spend time with God, it's always good to see where God is in your relationships and life. You know you are growing up in God when you can see Him working in everything. Maybe you are reading a book and something good happens to the main character that makes you happy, too. If you see that happening through God's eyes, He's showing you that you have His heart of love for others: "Laugh with your happy friends when they're happy; share tears when they're down" (Romans 12:14).

God is always teaching you and sharing Himself with you, but you need the Holy Spirit to see it. When God speaks to you, it helps you to understand even more of who He is and who you are. King David said that God was good to him even when he was going through valleys that he could get hurt in. David ended the psalm by saying, "Your beauty and love chase after me every day of my life. I'm back home in the house of God for the rest of my life" (Psalm 23:6). When you stop and reflect on what God's doing in your life and ask Him what He wants to show you, you give Him an opportunity to love on you and teach you more.

Journal

_____

_____

_____

TEACHING POINT 18

GOD IS ALWAYS TEACHING YOU AND SHARING HIMSELF WITH YOU, CONTINUED...

When you read the Bible and understand how you can apply what you read to your own life, it means you are maturing in your relationship with God. Don't get discouraged if you don't see a lot happening. Just like growing up is a process, so too, is growing up with God! Paul told Timothy, "Don't let anyone put you down because you're young" (1 Timothy 4:12). Any person, no matter how young or old, can have an amazing relationship with God.

Journal

_____

_____

_____

_____

_____

_____

_____

_____

_____

_____

Question/Reflection

What are some ways you could spend more time with God and grow your friendship with Him?

_____

_____

_____

_____

_____

_____

_____

_____

_____

_____

_____

_____

_____

_____

GROWTH ACTIVITY

FOR YOU

Can you remember something that God showed you that perhaps you didn't understand? Maybe it was a dream or a vision, or maybe it was a parable in the Bible you still want to understand. Take the next five minutes to ask God again what He meant by it. Sometimes when He talks to you, it sounds just like your own thoughts. You can tell it's Him talking because it sounds kind and it's something He would want to tell just you, not everyone else.

_____

_____

_____

_____

_____

_____

_____

_____

GROWTH ACTIVITY

FOR YOUR GROUP

Everyone in the group: Think about one of the hard times you have been through and what God taught you through it. Take two minutes each to share the hard thing in one sentence.

For example:
"I broke my ankle and couldn't play soccer for a season."
"We had to move because of my dad's new job."
"I was bullied at school."
"I went on a mission trip and saw a lot of poor children."

Then after you share that one sentence, share what God taught you and how He grew you closer to Him through it.

Congratulations, now you are all teachers!

GROWTH PRAYER

God, help me to obey You when you ask me to do things even when it is hard sometimes.

Help me to know when You do something in me and through me because I want to see Your presence and Your love at work in my life.

Thank You for sharing Yourself with me.

Thank You for teaching me daily how to be like You and how to live an awesome life.

Amen!

Workbook
CHAPTER
7

CHILDREN'S TESTIMONY

Mordekai's Testimony, Age 8

One Friday night we went on a treasure hunt. Before we went out, we asked God who was on His heart and where He wanted us to go. I heard God tell me that we should go to Walmart. I saw a map of where in Walmart we needed to go, which was by the fish tanks.

We found a woman in that exact spot, and when we told her why we were there, she started crying. She was sad because her kid was going to go live with his dad instead of her. She felt like God didn't care about how bad that felt. We told her how God did care a lot—He showed us exactly where she would be standing and what she would be wearing. We were able to tell her about Jesus and about how much God loved her. She felt a lot happier after we prayed with her. The whole church was excited about what happened.

CHAPTER 7 STORY SYNOPSIS

Maria wants the main role in the musical more than anything she's ever wanted in her whole life. When she hears that Lucas's grandmother sold her house, it gives her even more faith that God is going to help her as well.

Brooke is sick when she comes to audition and can't sing. At first, Maria is happy because now she'll get the main role. Then she remembers what God showed her: loving people like Brooke is her destiny. She feels that loving Brooke is more important than getting the role, so she and Hartley walk over to Brooke and pray that she will be healed. Brooke is healed and gets the main part, but Maria doesn't care because she's done what God asked her to do. For the first time in her relationship with God, she understands what being a friend of God feels like.

YOUR GOAL IS TO LOVE

YOUR GOAL IS TO LOVE

There will always be a temptation to do better or outperform others, but that is not the goal of a Christian. Your goal is to love like Jesus, and sometimes that means putting other people's needs before your own.

"If you've gotten anything at all out of following Christ, if his love has made any difference in your life, if being in a community of the Spirit means anything to you, if you have a heart, if you care—then do me a favor: Agree with each other, love each other, be deep-spirited friends. Don't push your way to the front; don't sweet-talk your way to the top. Put yourself aside, and help others get ahead. Don't be obsessed with getting your own advantage. Forget yourselves long enough to lend a helping hand" (Philippians 2:1-4).

Maria could have been the star of the show, but she would have missed out on a friendship with Brooke for the sake of accomplishing her dream. Sometimes you can be so focused on yourself and achieving your goals that you forget to include the #1 goal—to love others! Can you imagine what sports would look like if we were still trying to win but cared about the other players as much as the game we were playing? It would change the atmosphere of sports!

Journal

_____

_____

_____

TEACHING POINT 19

YOUR GOAL IS TO LOVE, CONTINUED...

Only people who are growing up in God trust God enough to know that He cares about their dreams more than they do. You don't have to feel like it's only up to you to make things happen. God will do so much on your behalf, more than you could hope for or imagine (see Ephesians 3:20, MSG). You can feel peaceful about being happy to help others succeed and put their needs in front of your own. People without a relationship with God don't have this assurance that God will do amazing things for them, but we know God will come through for us. And when you know God is doing good things for you, you can give away positions and rewards. The way God's love works, the more you give away, the more you get from God!

Journal

_____

_____

_____

_____

_____

_____

_____

_____

Question/Reflection

Have you ever stopped doing something for yourself and focused on helping someone else instead? How did that feel?

_____

_____

_____

_____

_____

_____

_____

_____

_____

_____

_____

_____

_____

TAKE RISKS WITH WHAT YOU HEAR FROM GOD

TEACHING POINT 20

TAKE RISKS WITH WHAT YOU HEAR FROM GOD

There are times to take risks with your faith that aren't always convenient. It is worth taking a risk as a Christian to do something you think God has asked you to do. The worst that could happen is that nothing gets better, or your friends make fun of you. Think about this, though. Because your goal is love, people can have the opportunity to feel loved and connected to God through your obedience.

This is why it's so important to know what God is saying to you so you can go and do it straightaway. God always has really good reasons for asking us to obey. Sometimes we won't understand why He wants us to do or say things until we see the end result. We can trust Him. "God means what he says. What he says goes. His powerful Word is sharp as a surgeon's scalpel, cutting through everything, whether doubt or defense, laying us open to listen and obey. Nothing and no one is impervious (resistant) to God's Word. We can't get away from it—no matter what" (Hebrews 4:12-13).

Journal

_____

_____

_____

_____

TEACHING POINT 20

TAKE RISKS WITH WHAT YOU HEAR FROM GOD, CONTINUED...

Maria had to risk her opportunity to get the main role in the play by praying for Brooke. Brooke or her mom might have been mad at Maria's desire to bring a religious moment into a show choir. The director or other teachers might have judged Maria for praying for Brooke. Maria had pure motives, though. She wanted to see God move, and when she put her own wishes to one side and reached out to Brooke with God's love, she saw God come through.

Sometimes you can get in trouble for wanting to see God show up in your everyday life. There are people who will get mad at you for trying, but if your motive is love, it never fails. Jesus even tells people that they are blessed or favored whenever people misunderstand them for the sake of their faith. When you walk with God in His love, or obey God, you can't help but feel His friendship. Love always wins!

Journal

_____

_____

_____

_____

_____

Question/Reflection

Have you ever obeyed what you thought Jesus was saying to do even though it was hard? If so, what happened?

_____
_____
_____
_____
_____
_____
_____
_____
_____
_____
_____
_____
_____

WHEN YOU OBEY GOD AND WALK WITH HIM, YOU CAN'T HELP BUT FEEL HIS FRIENDSHIP

TEACHING POINT 21

WHEN YOU OBEY GOD AND WALK WITH HIM, YOU CAN'T HELP BUT FEEL HIS FRIENDSHIP

Jesus said to the disciples that obedience is even better than service. When you learn how to follow Him as a friend, then you truly know Him. Paul knew this. He said to his friends: "You're looking at this backward. The issue in Jerusalem is not what they do to me . . . but what the Master Jesus does through my obedience. Can't you see that?" (Acts 21:13) He knew how good God was and trusted Him completely.

Jesus wants us to know everything about Him at a heart-to-heart level! Paul even prayed over the Ephesians: "I ask—ask the God of our Master, Jesus Christ, the God of glory—to make you intelligent and discerning in knowing him personally, your eyes focused and clear, so that you can see exactly what it is he is calling you to do, grasp the immensity of this glorious way of life he has for his followers, oh, the utter extravagance of his work in us who trust him—endless energy, boundless strength!" (Ephesians 1:17-18) Doing life with Jesus is glorious. When you know Him personally and trust Him, He gives you boundless energy and strength!

Journal

_____

_____

_____

_____

TEACHING POINT 21, CONTINUED...

WHEN YOU OBEY GOD AND WALK WITH HIM, YOU CAN'T HELP BUT FEEL HIS FRIENDSHIP, CONTINUED...

Even when hard things happen, friends of God know that God will find a way to bring good things out of the difficult times. People who aren't friends with God don't have that promise, so it's harder for them to take big risks that may not pay off. To them, failure means loss. For you, even when you lose, God works it out for your gain!

Journal

_____

_____

_____

_____

_____

_____

_____

_____

_____

_____

_____

Question/Reflection

How has God done good things in your heart and life after hard times or pain?

_____

_____

_____

_____

_____

_____

_____

_____

_____

_____

_____

_____

_____

_____

GROWTH ACTIVITY

FOR YOU

Increase your conversations with God by talking to Him for a minute or two seven times a day for seven days. When you wake up, talk to God as if He's your best friend (because He is). Tell Him about what you are going to do that day and that you're happy He'll be with you while you do it all. Talk to Him before you sit down to eat, or when you get done with school or church. Talk to Him about your relationships and life. Right before you go to bed, tell God about what you loved throughout the day and see if there was any way you loved like Jesus. Ask Him to help you grow.

GROWTH ACTIVITY

FOR YOUR GROUP

Pray together and ask God for a risk you could take in sharing something from His heart for someone in your life who doesn't know Him. Maybe you could write a card or a letter to a relative, or call a friend. Maybe invite someone over you don't know well and share your faith with him or her. Maybe pray for someone who is having a hard time. Make a plan and write it down. Next time you get together, report what happened! If nothing happened and all that you did was make a plan, congrats anyway—you are learning how to include other people you wouldn't normally hang out with.

GROWTH PRAYER

God, help my goal in life be to love—to love You, myself, and the world around me!

Help me to take risks to love people and hear Your heart.

Thank You that when I obey what You tell me to do, I can feel Your friendship.

Help me to see what Your will is and who I am supposed to love!

Amen!

Workbook
CHAPTER
8

CHILDREN'S TESTIMONY

D'Shawn's Testimony, Age 8

I was praying in my room and heard God tell me that my daddy would be home for Christmas. He was away with the army in another country called Afghanistan. My mom didn't know if she could believe me, and she told me Daddy wasn't supposed to come back until the next summer. Then, after Thanksgiving, my daddy surprised us by coming home early, and he got us good! His whole troop got to come home for Christmas and he doesn't have to go away from us again. I was able to tell my daddy that Jesus told me he was coming home for a Christmas present.

CHAPTER 8 STORY SYNOPSIS

Jeffrey, the bully, begins to pick on kids after school one day. Lucas prays for help and hears the Holy Spirit tell him to talk to Jeffrey one-on-one, on behalf of Jamal. God shows Lucas His heart for Jeffrey. Lucas feels that perhaps Jeffrey is going through some of the same problems at home that Jamal is going through. Lucas is filled with compassion for Jeffrey, which helps Lucas show Jeffrey that he cares about his pain. He appeals to Jeffrey and tells him that God doesn't want Jeffrey's life to be hard, that He loves him, and that He can help him. He also asks him to leave Jamal alone. Jeffrey agrees to back down.

That night, Lucas parents share that they have been praying about adopting another boy, and ask Lucas if he would consider welcoming Jamal into their family. He shares his word with them from last year's summer camp about the word brother."

YOUR FRIENDSHIP WITH GOD EVEN HELPS THOSE WHO DON'T KNOW HIM!

TEACHING POINT 22

YOUR FRIENDSHIP WITH GOD EVEN HELPS THOSE WHO DON'T KNOW HIM!

As Lucas invested time and friendship in Jamal, Jamal became more confident, very focused, and a great contributor to their friendship group. Your friendship with God will even help people who don't know Him to behave differently. Your friendship with God and your character that God grows in you actually help people around you to grow as well.

"Use your heads as you live and work among outsiders. Don't miss a trick. Make the most of every opportunity. Be gracious in your speech. The goal is to bring out the best in others in a conversation, not put them down, not cut them out" (Colossians 4:5-6). When you include others and let them know that you see good things in them, they can feel the love of God filling up their hearts.

Journal

_____

_____

_____

_____

_____

_____

TEACHING POINT 22

YOUR FRIENDSHIP WITH GOD EVEN HELPS THOSE WHO DON'T KNOW HIM! CONTINUED...

In other words, your life gives others opportunities to know what God is like because the more time you spend with God, the more you start to act like Him. God is doing things in you that affect the world around you in great ways. You get to bring out the best in others around you when you love them like God does. Your goals for your life are different. When you put the love in your heart into conversations and daily activities, you change the atmosphere around you. That atmosphere of love changes people's lives.

"We have three things to do.... Trust steadily in God, hope unswervingly, love extravagantly. And the best of the three is love" (1 Corinthians 13:13). "I tell you, love your enemies. Help and give without expecting a return. You'll never—I promise—regret it. Live out this God-created identity the way our Father lives toward us, generously and graciously, even when we're at our worst. Our Father is kind; you be kind" (Luke 6:35-36).

Journal

_____

_____

_____

_____

Question/Reflection

How has God's love from other people helped your heart? Can you imagine how other people's hearts could fill up on His love when you love them like Jesus even if they don't know Him?

_____

_____

_____

_____

_____

_____

_____

_____

_____

_____

_____

_____

YOU CAN BLESS OTHERS BY GIVING AWAY WHAT GOD HAS GIVEN YOU

TEACHING POINT 23

YOU CAN BLESS OTHERS BY GIVING AWAY WHAT GOD HAS GIVEN YOU

The word "impart" means to spiritually give away or reproduce—like making a copy of a picture on a copy machine. The compassion Lucas felt for Jamal and Jeffrey was given to him by God. He was able to appeal to Jeffrey in a way that made Jeffrey feel like Lucas understood what he was going through. God's love can feel like this sometimes. When Lucas shared about Jamal's situation, Jeffrey believed him because Lucas was speaking with compassion instead of anger.

You can communicate the things God is doing in you and showing you. You can share the Holy Spirit in you with Christians when you pray for them and give away what God has given you. You can bless the world around you with your ideas, thoughts, beliefs, love, culture, and more. Jesus was constantly imparting His ideas to the crowds who gathered around Him—ideas of what heaven was like, what God was like, and what life should be like. "When two of you get together on anything at all on earth and make a prayer of it, my Father in heaven goes into action. And when two or three of you are together because of me, you can be sure that I'll be there" (Matthew 18:19-20).

Journal

_____

_____

_____

YOU CAN BLESS OTHERS BY GIVING AWAY WHAT GOD HAS GIVEN YOU, CONTINUED...

Jesus showed people that God isn't a huge, mean God who is mad at people and is always judging them. He showed everyone that God is a loving, kind Father who cares a lot about everyone's interests.

When God shows you something, it is never just for you, although you might be the main one impacted by what you see. He does something for you so that He can do something through you that can affect your family, friends, and life. For Lucas, that meant that the "brothers" promise he was pursuing with Jamal was actually an answer to his parents' prayers to have another son. Their hearts opened to Jamal because of Lucas's deliberate friendship with him.

Journal

_____

_____

_____

_____

_____

_____

_____

Question/Reflection

If you think about the ideas and thoughts you've already come up with in your times with God, which ones do you know were ideas and thoughts given to you by God? Can you see how God could use some of them to help make other people's lives better?

_____

_____

_____

_____

_____

_____

_____

_____

_____

_____

GOD
BRINGS SOMETHING GOOD
OUT OF EVERYTHING

TEACHING
POINT
24

GOD BRINGS SOMETHING GOOD OUT OF EVERYTHING

God is so good. He loves to work everything out so that it benefits your life and your heart even the hardest things. "The moment we get tired in the waiting, God's Spirit is right alongside helping us along … He knows us far better than we know ourselves….and keeps us present before God. That's why we can be so sure that every detail in our lives of love for God is worked into something good" (Romans 8:26-28).

Even when something looks bad or when someone is mean to you, God helps you to look at the evil in other people as an opportunity to show more love. God helps you to make this evil bow down to His love in your life. He starts a plan to work good out of this. You always get a happy ending to the wrong that has been done to you, either on earth or when you get to heaven.

Journal

_____

_____

_____

_____

_____

_____

_____

TEACHING
POINT
24

GOD BRINGS SOMETHING GOOD OUT OF EVERYTHING, CONTINUED

For Maria, her calling to act gave Harper the opportunity to act, too, because they pursued Maria's word with more purpose. Harper was able to be in a commercial, too. Their actions also brought Brooke into a personal relationship with Jesus.

"So, what do you think? With God on our side like this, how can we lose?" (Romans 8:31)

Journal

_____

_____

_____

_____

_____

_____

_____

_____

_____

_____

Question/Reflection

Can you see where God has brought something good out of some of the sad things that have happened in your life?

_____

_____

_____

_____

_____

_____

_____

_____

_____

_____

_____

_____

_____

GROWTH ACTIVITY

FOR YOU

Pick two people in your life who seem to be hard to talk to, or who are going through a hard time. Now imagine what they could be like if they were connected to God's heart of love. Pray for that to happen. Write a letter to them that you might never deliver, but it still is a way of praying for them. In the letter, tell them about all the good qualities and gifts you see in them, and what you think God would say or is saying to them. Draw or write out what you think they are called to be, and point out the value God has for them.

1 _____

_____

_____

_____

_____

_____

_____

_____

2 _____

_____

_____

_____

_____

_____

_____

_____

GROWTH ACTIVITY

FOR YOUR GROUP

Share stories of when you were given something, but it wasn't just for you—it benefited your family, friends, or even school. What is something you believe God is going to give you that will affect more than just you? Now think about Joseph (in the Bible) and ask God how each person in the group is going to have a life that helps the world.

GROWTH PRAYER

God, I pray that my friendship with You will help people who don't even know you connect to You.

Help me share what You are doing in my heart to others.

Help me to trust that You will bring good things out of everything in my life, even when it is hard.

Show me how to see things through Your eyes so I can see what You are doing and stay encouraged and hopeful.

Amen!

Workbook
CHAPTER
9

CHILDREN'S TESTIMONY

Basha's Testimony, Age 8

God spoke to me in a dream to not be afraid. In the dream, there were dinosaurs chasing me and my family. We got chased into sinking sand (quicksand), and that's when Jesus showed up and turned the sand into water so we could swim out. God showed me that no matter what happens, He will always be there to protect me.

CHAPTER 9 STORY SYNOPSIS

Brooke has now become a Christian, and she and her family are going to the same church as her new friends. Brooke has a wonderful casting opportunity based on the musical they were in, but she doesn't know what to wear. At Sunday school, the pastor told them God wants to talk to them about everything, so she wants God to tell her what to wear and how to look for the casting director. She isn't hearing anything and is discouraged. Harper and Maria explain to her that God doesn't want to direct her on everything she does. He loves watching her choose because when she's happy being herself, she makes God look amazing. Brooke realizes that she never has to perform for God.

Maria and Harper go with Brooke to her audition so she can feel supported by their friendship. The casting director likes all three of them and lets them all audition. They all get a real acting part in a commercial. Maria's word is coming true. They end up worshiping together because they're so happy.

GOD SPEAKS OUT OF RELATIONSHIP AND GROWS YOUR FRIENDSHIP WITH HIM

TEACHING POINT 25

GOD SPEAKS OUT OF RELATIONSHIP AND GROWS YOUR FRIENDSHIP WITH HIM

God loves talking to you, but you won't understand Him if you don't get to know Him. God loves to talk to you and tell you what is in His heart. Hearing a prophetic word or just knowing the Bible is not enough. You have to know Him! You have to have a friendship connection with him. Have you ever had friends you knew so well, you knew what they were thinking the moment that you watched a funny scene in a movie together? You have inside jokes and a friendship connection that have been built out of your history together. God wants to make history with you!

"I'm speaking to you as dear friends" (Luke 12:4). "People who don't know God and the way he works fuss over these things, but you know both God and how he works. Steep yourself in God-reality, God-initiative, God-provisions. You'll find all your everyday human concerns will be met. Don't be afraid of missing out. You're my dearest friends! The Father wants to give you the very kingdom itself" (Luke 12:29-32). Spend time with God. Talk to Him, listen to Him, and be ready to notice things He points out to you in your day. Write down your prayers and what He says about them in a journal. Spend time outside and ask Him about His creation. See if any numbers or words stand out, and ask Him why.

Journal

_____

_____

TEACHING POINT 25

GOD SPEAKS OUT OF RELATIONSHIP AND GROWS YOUR FRIENDSHIP WITH HIM, CONTINUED...

Every moment you spend connecting with God helps that connection to grow. Every time you practice hearing Him and seeing what He shows you, you learn how to see and hear more clearly. It's what God has always wanted—to be your best friend and share everything about Himself with you.

Journal

_____

_____

_____

_____

_____

_____

_____

_____

_____

_____

_____

Question/Reflection

If you were going to give yourself a score out of ten, how much would you say you know Jesus right now? What could you do to know Him more?

_____
_____
_____
_____
_____
_____
_____
_____
_____
_____
_____
_____
_____

WHEN GOD ISN'T SPEAKING, IT IS BECAUSE HE WANTS YOU TO GROW IN YOUR IDENTITY

TEACHING
POINT
26

WHEN GOD ISN'T SPEAKING, IT IS BECAUSE HE WANTS YOU TO GROW IN YOUR IDENTITY

God speaks sometimes to share His heart with you, instruct you, amuse you, help you, connect to you, or encourage you. Over time, your friendship with Him matures and you start to understand exactly who He made you to be. This is called building your personal identity with God. Your identity is the sum of who you are. When you know yourself, you know what you are good at, what you enjoy, how you see things, how you communicate with others, and what your personality type is. You know how to pursue the great things in life, not just settle for good things. You do life out of your whole self, not just the parts you think people want to see.

You also choose to do wonderful things out of your own free will. This was God's design all along—to have mature sons and daughters who do things and go places because it's a natural part of who they are. He's never wanted to boss you around. The more mature you become, the less you need instruction or direction. You just know what to do. Some people are waiting for God to talk to them and tell them what to do about everything—even what to eat for lunch! This usually happens because they don't know who they are, and they don't know God all that well yet, either.

Journal

_____

_____

_____

WHEN GOD ISN'T SPEAKING, IT IS BECAUSE HE WANTS YOU TO GROW IN YOUR IDENTITY, CONTINUED...

God trusted Paul to choose where he wanted to be: "As long as I'm alive in this body, there is good work for me to do. If I had to choose right now, I hardly know which I'd choose. Hard choice! . . . I plan to be around awhile, companion to you as your growth and joy in this life of trusting God continues" (Philippians 1:22-25). Paul said, "Live freely, animated and motivated by God's Spirit" (Galatians 5:16). You have the freedom to make all the choices you want. It brings God glory when you make great choices. It makes His character in you look so beautiful. He doesn't always tell you what to do because He wants to show the world that you are powerful and you have chosen a life in Him that is strong and empowered!

Journal

_____

_____

_____

_____

_____

_____

Question/Reflection

Jesus wants you to know yourself—what you like, how you like it, what your character strengths are, what your personality is like, and how you do things. Why do you think He cares so much about helping you be you?

_____

_____

_____

_____

_____

_____

_____

_____

_____

_____

_____

WHEN YOU ACT LIKE JESUS WITH YOUR FRIENDS, THERE IS ALWAYS A BENEFIT

TEACHING
POINT
27

WHEN YOU ACT LIKE JESUS WITH YOUR FRIENDS, THERE IS ALWAYS A BENEFIT

The beautiful thing about real relationships is that you help each other become better people. Your times of connecting aren't just for fun and companionship. You become more of your true, God-given self as you spend time with the right people. A young girl we know began to help autistic kids who were in a program that ran alongside their art class at school. She got kids to volunteer and she paired each one with an autistic kid for the art class. Through this amazing program, all of her friends learned how amazing these children who had autism were. She helped give dignity and understanding to kids who were sometimes ignored or forgotten. In her school today, most of the kids now have autistic friends, and there is very little stigma on being autistic. Your promises from God even affect your family and friends, and they add to what God is showing you.

Journal

_____

_____

_____

_____

_____

_____

TEACHING POINT 27

WHEN YOU ACT LIKE JESUS WITH YOUR FRIENDS, THERE IS ALWAYS A BENEFIT, CONTINUED...

"So let's do it—full of belief, confident that we're presentable inside and out. Let's keep a firm grip on the promises that keep us going. He always keeps his word. Let's see how inventive we can be in encouraging love and helping out . . . spurring each other on" (Hebrews 10:22-25). You actually are supposed to be creative and inventive in your life and relationships! Remember that Brooke's friendship with Maria and Harper meant they unexpectedly got to act in a commercial with her. You being you in your strength, personality, and relationship with God actually helps your friends have open doors to opportunities, too. Greatness happens when Jesus is in the center of your friendships!

As you grow up in God, you start to see how being a part of His family actually gives you other opportunities that you would have never had. You all can't help but help each other achieve great things and be great people!

Journal

_____

_____

_____

_____

_____

Question/Reflection

Some kids find that the more they know God, the easier it is to make choices that benefit not just themselves, but the people around them, too. Would you agree? Why/why not?

_____

_____

_____

_____

_____

_____

_____

_____

_____

_____

GROWTH ACTIVITY

FOR YOU

Make a list of the fruits of the Holy Spirit you'd like to grow in, and write at least three of these words down. For example: patience, peace, love, happiness, self-control, humility, sharing, and selflessness. Then ask God to show you each time you might have an opportunity to grow during the week and write it down next to the word. We grow when we see our need to grow!

1
_____
_____
_____
_____
_____

2
_____
_____
_____
_____

3
_____
_____
_____
_____
_____
_____
_____
_____
_____

GROWTH ACTIVITY

FOR YOUR GROUP

Discuss what choices people in the group are good at making—decisions they don't need help with, but someone else facing the same situation might. What are things that they can do right now without adult help because they have skill and training? Celebrate one accomplishment of each person in the group . . . and show photos, medals, short videos, etc. if you have them. Then encourage each other about those accomplishments even if they happened several years ago.

GROWTH PRAYER

God, I pray that You would help me discover my identify more and more.

Help me to walk in the character of this great identity.

Thank You for trusting me to make some important decisions, and I pray that I would feel Your heart of joy when I make them.

Also, help my relationships benefit from my relationship with You.

Amen!

Workbook
CHAPTER
10

CHILDREN'S TESTIMONY

Hailey's Testimony, Age 10

When I first started hearing from God, my parents and I were learning together. Kind of a funny story: I have a fish in a small tank on my desk. It died and my mom and dad replaced it with one that looks just like it, but did not tell me. One night, I had a dream that my fish had died and been replaced without me knowing. I got up and told my mom my dream, and she looked at me weird and asked, "God gave you that dream?" Then she said, "Hailey, we did replace your fish with one that looks just like your old one, but we did not tell you because we did not want you to be sad." I felt sad about my fish, but my parents explained that God was teaching them that God speaks to kids just like He speaks to adults. I think God is teaching my parents more about my gift than me.

CHAPTER 10 STORY SYNOPSIS

The kids are in kids' church, listening to the pastor share his message. He is sharing about how the Holy Spirit reveals the deepest parts of the heart of God to our hearts and ties them together. He does this so that we can hear from God and feel what He feels and know what He knows. He shares how his parents, who have been married a long time, use fewer words while they're working together in the kitchen. He says that's because they know each other and love each other so well.

Harper and Maria feel that way about their friendship. Then Jamal tells Lucas that he has made him feel this way, too. It's made Jamal think maybe there really is a God, and he wants to grow up in God, too! The four friends pray for him with the pastor, and Jamal invites Jesus to be his friend.

At Maria's house that summer, they notice Hartley practicing how to listen to God as well. They discover that you don't have to wait for a meeting or church to grow up with God. It happens every day for any kid who wants to know Him.

YOU CAN LOVE WELL

TEACHING
POINT
28

YOU CAN LOVE WELL

You are called to love people just like God sent Jesus to love them. This love has an invitation in it, not a command. You can't force anyone to believe what you believe, but you do get to love them. Regardless of their beliefs, they are worthy of love!

Jesus treated all the people around Him as if they were worthy of going to heaven, whether they believed in Him or not. He loved them as though they had full value! This is how you are supposed to love! You can try and share your faith, but you aren't responsible to actually get people saved. Only God can do that. What you do get to be, though, is an example of His love.

"This is how much God loved the world: He gave his Son, his one and only Son. And this is why: so that no one need be destroyed; by believing in him, anyone can have a whole and lasting life. God didn't go to all the trouble of sending his Son merely to point an accusing finger, telling the world how bad it was. He came to help, to put the world right again" (John 3:16-17). You don't get to condemn anyone for not believing, but you can treat him or her like family.

Journal

_____

_____

_____

_____

TEACHING POINT 28, CONTINUED...

TEACHING POINT 28

YOU CAN LOVE WELL, CONTINUED...

Sometimes you love God so much that you want everyone around you to know how good He is, but instead of building relationships and friendships with people, you just preach to them. That doesn't help anyone most of the time because people will connect to God's love through you before you even use words. Once they feel as if they can trust you and you feel like a friend to them, then you get to share. The more you are growing up with God, the more you grow in love for others. People can feel that love in real ways, and they will connect to you more because of it even if they don't agree with your beliefs.

Journal

_____

_____

_____

_____

_____

_____

_____

_____

_____

186 GROWING UP WITH GOD

Question/Reflection

When you think of people who show you God's love, how do they show it? Is it through preaching or through treating you in a certain way?

_____

_____

_____

_____

_____

_____

_____

_____

_____

_____

_____

_____

_____

THE NUMBER-ONE WAY PEOPLE BECOME CHRISTIANS IS THROUGH RELATIONSHIP

THE NUMBER-ONE WAY PEOPLE BECOME CHRISTIANS IS THROUGH RELATIONSHIP

People will come to Jesus through your relationship with them. Sometimes churches go out and do wonderful evangelism outreaches, or cook a meal and give it to the homeless, or travel to other countries on school evangelism trips. These are important, but the primary way you are called to share your faith is to do it every day through your love.

"God is love. When we take up permanent residence in a life of love, we live in God and God lives in us. This way, love has the run of the house, becomes at home and mature in us, so that we're free of worry on Judgment Day—your standing in the world is identical with Christ's. There is no room in love for fear. Well-formed love banishes fear. Since fear is crippling, a fearful life—fear of death, fear of judgment—is one not yet fully formed in love. We, though, are going to love—love and be loved. First we were loved, now we love. He loved us first" (1 John 4:17-19).

Journal

_____

_____

_____

_____

_____

_____

TEACHING POINT 29

THE NUMBER-ONE WAY PEOPLE BECOME CHRISTIANS IS THROUGH RELATIONSHIP, CONTINUED...

Jesus said that to really grow up in God, you need to do two things: "The first in importance is, 'Listen, Israel: The Lord your God is one; so love the Lord God with all your passion and prayer and intelligence and energy.' And here is the second: 'Love others as well as you love yourself'" (Mark 12:29-30). Think about that. You like to make sure you get enough to eat, rides to your friends' houses, and help from your friends and family when you need it. When you love others as well as you love yourself, you spend as much time making sure their needs are met as you do your own.

When you live in love for God, people can feel that you are living differently. You get to invite people to see God by the way you love. When they experience love through you every single day for months, and even years, it makes them know for sure that God's love is real!

Journal

_____

_____

_____

_____

_____

_____

Question/Reflection

What do you think is the main thing your family and friends need from you? How much of it do you need Jesus's help with?

_____

_____

_____

_____

_____

_____

_____

_____

_____

_____

_____

_____

_____

_____

YOU GROW IN GOD EVERY DAY

YOU GROW IN GOD EVERY DAY

You don't have to grow just in a few spurts at meetings, church, or camps. You get to grow every day through how you make choices. You will know you are growing in God by the changes that happen in your heart! Just like fruit trees grow fruit every year, your life will start to have character and you'll feel comfortable and happy being you. You will have the ability to really know what God is saying to you, and people around you will benefit from all that spiritual fruit. You will be able to measure how different you are because you will have characteristics of God's love.

Paul explained how to check if you are growing: "But what happens when we live God's way? He brings gifts into our lives, much the same way that fruit appears in an orchard—things like affection for others, exuberance about life, serenity. We develop a willingness to stick with things, a sense of compassion in the heart, and a conviction that a basic holiness permeates things and people. We find ourselves involved in loyal commitments, not needing to force our way in life, able to marshal and direct our energies wisely" (Galatians 5:22-23).

Journal

_____

_____

_____

_____

TEACHING POINT 30

YOU GROW IN GOD EVERY DAY, CONTINUED...

You will have the fruits of the Spirit, and there's nothing God loves more than giving that fruit away to the hungry. The more they get to taste of His love and kindness through His people, the more they'll want. They'll know that it's the kind of love that doesn't come from people. It's a heavenly love. "I'm spreading a banquet of Tree-of-Life fruit, a supper plucked from God's orchard" (Revelation 2:7). Even if you find it hard to love people now, God's love will fill your heart so much that it will grow ten sizes bigger and then you'll find it easy to be just like Jesus.

Journal

_____

_____

_____

_____

_____

_____

_____

_____

_____

_____

Question/Reflection

How long do you think it takes to grow up in God so much that you end up being just like Jesus? God grows some things quickly and other things slowly. How do you know if you are growing up in God already? Do you know He loves you just as much now as He will when you have grown up in Him? That's how amazing His love is.

GROWTH ACTIVITY

FOR YOU

LOVE LETTER WEEK: Write down a spiritual note, encouragement, or letter for each person in your family that they can read quickly each day for seven days. Post them on the bathroom mirror or fridge, or even leave some on their pillows. Try and encourage them with a Scripture, and tell them something you love about them.

GROWTH ACTIVITY

FOR YOUR GROUP

Break up into groups of two. Share your faith with the other person as if he or she doesn't know Jesus. Try and be as real and heartfelt as possible. Then pray with the person to receive Jesus (please refer to page 200 if you need the tool).

GROWTH PRAYER

God, teach me how to love well. I pray that as I love people, they will get to know You.

I pray that some will become Christians because of Your love for me and my love for You!

Please help me to grow daily with You.

Amen!

PRAY TO BECOME A CHRISTIAN PRAYER

Father, You loved the world so much that You sent Jesus to die for the sins of the whole world—everything we've done wrong. Then You raised Jesus back to life to give us life. I receive Your forgiveness and Your new life that You give me. You call me Your child, and I call You my Lord. You washed me clean and made me right with God. I don't have to feel bad anymore about what I've done wrong! I welcome Your Holy Spirit in my life. Your gift of power for me to live a new life, like Jesus, and to have a close relationship with You. Thank You and I love You!

Amen

We included this prayer so that you can lead your friends to Jesus, too.

Shawn grew up in a passionately Christian home with parents who were actively involved in his spiritual growth. Because of seeing how nurturing a relationship with God starts at a young age (Shawn and his wife, Cherie, both got saved at the age of three), he loves seeing the next generation empowered with tools that help them take their faith seriously.

Shawn is a best-selling author, conference and event speaker, TV host, and pastor in Los Angeles. Writing and telling stories are two of his favorite pastimes.

Lamont Hunt is an award-winning character animator and illustrator, currently living in the Los Angeles area. He grew up in Springfield, VA, and Memphis, TN, but most of his growing up was done in the Sioux Falls area of South Dakota. He went on to gain a BFA in drawing/illustration/graphic design at the University of Nebraska-Lincoln. Go Huskers! He gained more specialized education in animation at the Art Institute International, MN, Animation Mentor, and Animsquad. Lamont has worked as an artist/illustrator and animator in South Dakota, Minnesota, Taiwan, and California, and with companies like The Jim Henson Co. and Ken Duncan Studio. *Growing Up with God* is his first illustrated children's book.

GROWING UP WITH GOD
Study Course

Equip future generations with the life-changing tools they need to grow into all God has for them.

CHAPTER BOOK | WORKBOOK | COLORING BOOK
TEACHER'S GUIDE | 10 DVD SESSIONS

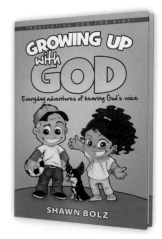  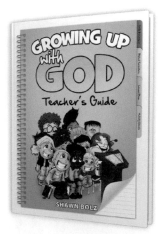 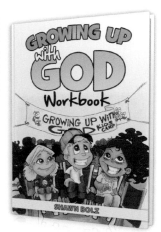

Ideal for use in Sunday school, VBS, small groups, and homeschool settings.

Parent tips included in each chapter!

BUY THE STUDY COURSE ON
GrowingupwithGod.com

GROWING UP WITH GOD
Coloring Book

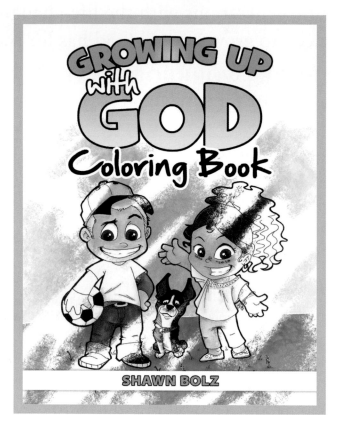

Growing Up with God has a coloring book!

In *Growing Up with God*, Lucas, Maria, and their friends spend the year on a journey of listening to God's heart of love. Through it, they learn how to support and believe in themselves and everyone around them. In this coloring book, your kids will experience the satisfaction of adding vibrant colors to the artwork of renowned character design and animation expert, Lamont Hunt. Along the way, they'll be reminded of the life lessons shared in the chapter book.

This coloring book is awaiting your child's unique passion to color these characters to life.

growingupwithgod.com

GROWING UP WITH GOD
Chapter Book

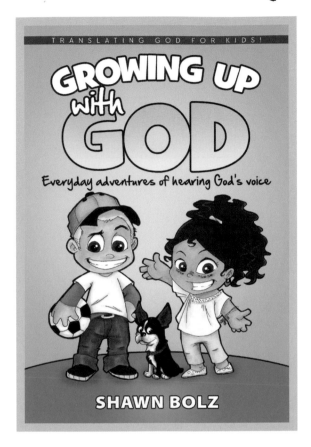

Join Lucas and Maria and friends on their everyday adventures in friendship with God!

Lucas knows God talks to him, but he would have never imagined that he would hear such a specific thing about his year . . . and could Maria really have heard God about her destiny? They both have to wonder if God speaks to kids this way. Over the months that follow, God begins to connect them to other kids that grow into friends. Who could have guessed that by the end of the year, their lives would be so exciting!

Award-winning illustrator Lamont Hunt illustrates the rich, vibrant God journey of kids you can relate to. By best-selling author Shawn Bolz.

Growing Up with God is an amazing adventure!

growingupwithgod.com